Signs of The Times

A selection of comic signs from 'The Times Diary'

ELM TREE BOOKS

Elm Tree/ Hamish Hamilton

First published in Great Britain 1974
by Elm Tree Books Ltd
90 Great Russell Street, London WC1
Copyright © 1974 by Times Newspapers Ltd.

SBN 241 89162 0

Printed photolitho in Great Britain by
Ebenezer Baylis and Son, Limited,
The Trinity Press, Worcester, and London

FOREWORD

The belief that *The Times* is a staid and stuffy newspaper is held only by those unfamiliar with it. Reputations die hard. It may never have been such a newspaper, and certainly it is not now. Yet there are, no doubt, people who are convinced that it still devotes its front page entirely to advertisements, as it did until surprisingly recently. (There are also those who think it should never have changed, but that is another story.)

The Times Diary was introduced at the same time as the front page was switched to news. Its function is to provide relief from the serious and responsible reporting which surrounds it. In doing so, it relies quite heavily on its readers, who submit anecdotes, newspaper clippings and other ephemera which strike them as funny and worth sharing.

The road sign saga began by accident. Adam Roberts of Islington sent me a picture of the sign which guides motorists through the Byzantine one-way system at Barnsbury, and suggested I should run a contest for the most confusing road sign. One Monday in May I printed the picture and Roberts's suggestion. By one of those coincidences of which great series are made, the same morning—too soon for it to have been a response to the invitation—I received another photograph in the post. This was a juxtaposition of a sign reading 'Public Conveniences' with one saying 'Limit 2 Tons'—the first of many lavatory jokes I received, although I did not use many.

But I used that one and, once you have two pictures on successive days, a series is born. Soon pictures began pouring in at a rate of about six a day. Of these, perhaps one in six would be funny enough to publish. Still, if we could maintain a rate of five usable signs a week, the series could continue indefinitely.

I am consistently amazed by the peculiar habits of readers. There are, it seems, large numbers of them who go round the country taking pictures of road signs. And not just in this country. Photographs came from Tanzania, Tonga, Sri Lanka—any place that somebody had put up an ambiguous or quaintly worded sign, it seemed, there was a reader of *The Times* to snap it.

As the series continued into the holiday season, people began taking new pictures specially for it. Themes recurred. Apart from the lavatories, there was a strong line in cemetery jokes—No Through Road was a favourite. Entries from Africa had a zoological streak— 'Elephants have right of way' was the best. A number of readers who had taken their holidays in Cyprus when it was possible to do so sent pictures of signs warning that roads were slippery with grape juice.

Towards the end I began to suspect that people were inventing signs themselves and taking pictures of them. Anything which looked as though it had been faked was rejected. As I write, the series is continuing, but the world's supply of funny road signs cannot be inexhaustible.

Every newspaper is known for something. The *Daily Mirror* has Andy Capp, *The Sun* has pictures of undressed women, *The Guardian* has punning headlines and *The Times* has road signs. At least, he said, running for cover, nobody can accuse us of being pedestrian.

Michael Leapman
Editor of *The Times Diary*

This bewildering road sign was photographed near Leigh-on-Sea, Essex, by G. J. Collier of Hove.

I. T. Cook of Brightlingsea photographed this unusual combination of signs near Chelmsford, Essex, where they apparently breed very fast horses.

This stern sign, apparently an invitation to mass suicide, was photographed on the banks of the River Swale at Richmond, Yorkshire, by Michael King of Hampton Hill, Middlesex.

Professor Brian Simpson of the University of Kent took this picture in Italy where, as you can see, the rabbits are so big and menacing that they build themselves brick warrens.

This road sign, a realistic bowing to the inevitable, was photographed in Uganda by Sir James Cook of Budleigh Salterton.

In Kisumu, Kenya, it appears that road markings are painted by one-armed men with bowlers, as shown in this photograph taken by Hugh McClintock.

Aubrey Benn of Hendon photographed this road sign at the entrance to the old bomber base at Hethel, Norfolk. It serves to confirm the legends of what servicemen used to eat, and suggests that the end of the war took the quartermaster by surprise.

RHINOS
PLEASE REMAIN IN
YOUR VEHICLE

RENOSTERS
BLY ASSEBLIEF IN U
VOERTUIG

This ambiguous road sign was photographed in the Transvaal, South Africa, by Sandra Virgo of Elstree.

Photographed in distant Tonga by J. V. Alexander of Bayswater, this road sign is clearly about to obey its own instruction.

Philip Gaskell of Trinity College, Cambridge, photographed this impressive road sign.

This complicated sign was found by Harold Knight of Finchley at the entrance to Chillon Castle, by Lake Geneva.

Peter N. Scott sent this picture from Switzerland where the frogs, like the people, are, as you see, meticulous time-keepers.

Adam Roberts sent this picture taken in Thornhill Road, Islington. He likened his own entry to a *Times* leader, which we could not be expected to agree with: 'It takes an unnecessarily long and circuitous route, veering first to the left and then several times decisively to the right, before ending up in a position which has the twin disadvantages of being definitely to the right of centre, and depressingly close to where the reader started off from anyway.'

Mrs. Lee Ayre of East Dulwich photographed this baffling sign in a real Japanese garden.

This worrying sign was photographed on a transformer station in south central France by R. J. Harrison Church.

A rather uncompromising sign photographed in Taunton by Alec Davis of Battersea.

ВЫХОД

WAY OUT

→

←EXIT

Mr. G. B. L. Wilson of Kew, who snapped this bewildering sign backstage at the Coliseum (where the Bolshoi Ballet appeared) thinks it might be a subtle invitation to defection.

This road sign is mystifying rather than confusing or ambiguous. Photographed by Dr. H. D. Juler at the Higher Ferry in Dartmouth, it presumably can apply only to Hovercraft.

Peter Evans of Hale, Cheshire, sent in this shot of a bewildering road sign at Padstow in Cornwall.

Many possibilities are left open by this negative road sign! It was snapped in Queensland by Brian Kemble of Hampstead Garden Suburb.

Lionel Humphrey of Salcombe, Devon, photographed this sign at the bottom of his road. He is not sure whether it is the hornets which make the toilets unsuitable for motor coaches or whether there is another reason.

This vivid message was photographed by Iain Scarlet of Kilburn in a North London Launderette.

The beauty of this road sign lies in the touching precision of the man who did the measuring. Arthur Rees of Bromsgrove, who photographed it, tells us the bridge in question is about a mile away.

An oddly placed sign photographed by M. A. Connolly of
Cambridge at Southbourne, Bournemouth. It clearly boasts
adventurous cyclists.

CATTLE & CALVES

TURN RIGHT

← PIGS

STRAIGHT ON

It seems unnecessarily cruel to cattle who have taken the trouble to learn to read, to try and confuse their sense of direction. The sign was photographed in the local market by Patricia Spicer of Lewes.

This careful sign, conveying all eventualities, was photographed at Watchet Harbour, Somerset, by Francis Stoner of Oxford.

Major D. P. Earlam of Salisbury snapped this graphic road sign in Kandy, Sri Lanka. The writing, he says, announces that it is a pedestrian crossing and the picture seems to be a warning of what could happen if the rules are not heeded.

This sign would seem to indicate that they do not see many hairpins in Lismore, Eire, where it was photographed by Deborah Cawse of Bristol.

An alarming pair of road signs photographed by John Walker of Basingstoke. He saw them near Horley in Surrey.

This admirably precise signpost was photographed in Ireland some
years ago by Richard Gibson of Holmes Chapel, Cheshire.

This contribution, from H. M. Williams of Tavistock, is to be seen
outside a car park near Virginia Water.

This warning of unknown peril was photographed in Derbyshire by Peter MacKeith of Pimlico.

Mr. H. R. Maule of Reading photographed this cordial road sign in Cornwall.

This comprehensive road sign was photographed in Kendal, Westmorland, by Martin Staple of Cardiff.

An anonymous reader photographed this graphic pair of road signs in Lusaka, Zambia.

This confusing road sign was spotted in Khartum and photographed by June Ingold of Hitchin.

This sign was photographed in Great Brickhill, Bucks., by David
Kessler of Bletchley. In these undisciplined times it provides a stern
reminder for us all.

This road sign, difficult to comply with, was photographed in Agra, India, by David Brewer of Hampstead.

Peggy Morris of Teddington found this amazing sign in Barmouth, Merioneth. We understand that it has been amended since.

Oswald Jones from Monmouthshire snapped this descriptive road sign in mid-Wales, about six years ago.

Adrian Bower of Birkenhead found this sign. Can there really never be any accidents?

Cemeteries are fertile ground for sign spotters, and this is a particularly happy juxtaposition. It was photographed in Streatham by Harry Ingham of Kensington.

This worrying sign was outside some rebuilding works at Oxford University. It was photographed by Robin Benn of Beaconsfield.

Roger Lubbock of Kensington photographed this sign near Bulawayo, Rhodesia. It is uninformative to the point of churlishness.

Dr. Marion Way of Quebec, Durham, photographed this uncordial sign at the Beamish Museum in Durham.

A well illustrated road sign photographed at John Brown's Shipyard at Clydebank by Richard Einzig of Wimbledon Park.

This rather indelicate sign in Perthshire was sent in by a Surrey
reader who wishes to remain anonymous.

Although these ducks do not look as menacing as the rabbits in Italy
(as shown in a previous photograph), the Dutch would seem to treat
them with reverence. This is an authorised duck crossing in Delft,
and we are told by Sir Peter Garren who photographed this sign that
'Let Op' means 'Caution' or 'Look out!'

John Miller of Selsdon found this sign near Burford.

Watch out for the stampede! This appropriately placed pair of signs
was photographed by John Hoschander of London and sent in by
F. G. Broadbent of Twickenham.